Eve's Angels

Bible Study

Eve's Angels® Bible Study

www.evesangels.org

.

First Edition Copyright © 2012 Anny Donewald
www.evesangels.org

Transcribed and Outlined by: Ari Davis and Erika Liechty
Editing and Formatting by: Michele Surdej

ISBN-13:978-1480299672

ISBN-10:1480299677

Scripture taken from the New American Standard Bible®,
Copyright© 1960, 1962, 1963, 1968, 1971, 1972, 1973,
1975, 1977, 1995 by the Lockman Foundation

Scripture taken from the Holy Bible, New International
Version® NIV® Copyright© 1973. 1978, 1984, 2010 by
Biblica, Inc. Used by permission. All rights reserved
worldwide.

Scripture take from the Holy Bible, English Standard
Version (ESV) is adapted from the Revised Standard
Version of the Bible, Copyright Division of Christian
Education of the National Council of the Churches of
Christ in the U.S.A. All rights reserved.

Dedication

This is dedicated to my daughter.

I hope you have these lessons so deep in your spirit, that you never have to wonder who you are or look for someone to answer that. I hope you follow God no matter what.

Always show other women what you know, but more importantly, Who you know.

He's with you, even when I'm not. I love you the most. I'm passing you the baton. You got this!

About the Author

Anny Donewald earned her bachelor's degree in Family Studies with a minor in Sociology from Western Michigan.

At the age of 19, Anny entered the sex industry. This decision directly impacted the next six years, and changed the course of her life forever. She was an exotic dancer in Chicago, Detroit, and other various cities across the country before landing in Las Vegas and California.

She was radically born again through an intervention of the Spirit of God and has given her life to the vision of setting people free from this darkness.

Table of Contents

Section Three

Section Four

Section Five

Section Six

Instructions for

Leaders

Leaders: This book is to be used in a group setting following the Eve's Angels framework. The leader should study the material before the bible studies and come with ideas and questions to the group. She should organize and personalize the material for the study group.

It is tailored for group discussion, not just a book to be read. Follow where the Holy Spirit is guiding the conversation. It is imperative that you go over the previous lesson from the last time you met, so the students can talk about what they learned and also discuss the encounters they had with God.

You need to review it to see if Holy Spirit did anything with it while they were away. Discussing it brings forth further revelation after they have had time to process.

These are more than teachings. These are new lenses to see the world out of. Each meeting week needs at least a ten minute introduction to see how people are seeing life and topics in a new way.

It is critical that you partner your students up with a mentor or leader to guide them through the weeks together. If a student comes in the middle of your session, have the mentor catch them of up for the weeks lost. Develop a system of discipleship for the girls that will attend the study.

HINTS:

- *Italicized words* typically are a hint to prompt you to answer a question. Answer on the space provided, as it is discussed together.
- ACT ON IT! This section is for you to do on your own time when the group is not meeting. Take time on your weeks off to study the Word, pray, and thoughtfully answer the questions. Please review and check in with the students to see how their homework went at the following meeting.

Instructions for

Students

Students:

We are so excited for you to start this study! If it is your first bible study, or if you have been doing this a long time, we are confident that you will grow in the Lord as you apply yourself to gaining understanding of God's Word, and deepening your personal relationship with Him. Be sure to connect with one of the leader's in your study group. They are there to walk with you through these lessons, as you learn together. It is tailored for group discussion, not just a book to be read. Follow where the Holy Spirit is guiding the conversation. Speak out in the group!

HINTS:

- *Italicized words* typically are a clue to prompt you to answer a question. Answer on the space provided, as it is discussed together.

- ACT ON IT! This section is for you to do on your own time when the group is not meeting. Take time on your weeks off to study the Word, pray, and thoughtfully answer the questions. The more you apply yourself, the more you will grow and change into the woman of God you were created to be!

Before you begin, take some time to pray and ask God to reveal Himself to you over these next months together.

We love you, and we are praying for you!

Introduction

This bible study was created out of a need. I was given a week's warning that God wanted me to launch Eve's Angels Bible Study and Outreach. I didn't have time to figure out what was working and what wasn't working for other groups, and so I did what I always do when I don't know what to do: I prayed. God answered. These topics are things the Lord has given me along the way. These are things I've had to walk out personally, things I have taught not only to girls in the sex industry, but Christian women around the country looking for answers to life. I'm not a biblical scholar, I'm not ordained, and I'm not certified. However, I am a Christian, and I hear from God, as He answers my prayers. I hope this study prompts questions, thoughts, and a new way of looking at different subjects that may have gone unnoticed before. Most importantly, I hope this draws you into a closer relationship with Jesus Christ. He's real; not just a book to be studied, but a Man to be known.

Blessings,

Anny Donewald
Founder
Eve's Angels Inc.

Eve's Angels

The Kingdom

The Kingdom

Week One: The Kingdom of Heaven

Jesus came to earth with a message. Contrary to popular belief, this message was not "You're a sinner!" or, "You're going to hell!" His message was "Repent, for the Kingdom of Heaven is near!" **(Matthew 3:2)** Jesus taught on many things, but the Kingdom was his main message.

Read Together Luke 17:20-21

The Kingdom of Heaven is a system that brings you into a new dimension of living. Just like there are systems on this Earth, there is a system of Heaven. There is a way things work there that supersedes the systems that are already in place here on Earth. We are to take the system of the Kingdom of Heaven, and infiltrate all the other systems. The school system is one such example.

What are some other systems of this world that you are involved in where the Kingdom needs to be established?

_____

_____

_____

_____

_____

_____

The Kingdom is a new dimension of living. Jesus is the King of Kings, and the Kingdom of Heaven is His domain. By stepping down from Heaven and modeling how the Kingdom can come to Earth, Jesus provided a way for us to enter the Kingdom and gave us the authority to bring the Kingdom to Earth. As citizens of the Kingdom, our job is to establish the Kingdom for the King's return. His Kingdom is a realm that supersedes the natural realm, so when you enter the Kingdom you begin to live a supernatural life.

Your citizenship as a Christian is rooted in the Kingdom of Heaven. Wherever your citizenship is, that is where your laws are. That is the government in which you have to abide by, because you belong to that system.

Read out loud the following scripture together as a group.

"As you go, proclaim this message: 'The Kingdom of Heaven has come near.' Heal the sick, raise the dead, cleanse those who have leprosy, drive out demons. Freely you have received; freely give." Matthew 10:7-8

You cannot physically see the Kingdom; it does not come through observation. For example, gravity governs the earthly realm and we operate according to the force of gravity even though we can't see it. In the same way we operate in the realm of the Kingdom despite lack of sight. You know that the Kingdom is here when supernatural things start to happen as people are changed and forgiven, healed and raised from the dead.

Have you ever "seen" the Kingdom come? How do you know? Discuss with your group.

_____

_____

_____

_____

_____

Jesus wants you to experience fully the Kingdom being brought here on this Earth. So get ready!

ACT ON IT!

- Pray about this scripture. **Matthew 6:33**
- What is God speaking to you?

_____

_____

_____

_____

The Kingdom is mentioned 104 times in the Bible. (Sometimes as the Kingdom of God, and sometimes as the Kingdom of Heaven. We assume them to be the same). Find some scriptures that are referring to His Kingdom.

- What is God speaking to you about the Kingdom?

_____

_____

_____

_____

The Kingdom

Week Two: World's Laws vs. Kingdom's Laws

The Kingdom is run in complete opposition to the world system. When we live according to our natural mind, the ways of the Kingdom do not make sense. Now that you are born in the Spirit, it is important that you learn how life in the Kingdom is done so you can manifest the Kingdom of Heaven.

1) The world says if you want to get something, do whatever is necessary to get it. In the Kingdom, if you want to get something, give it first.

Read and Write Out Luke 6:38

_____
_____
_____
_____
_____

Read and Write Out 2 Corinthians 9:10

_____
_____
_____
_____
_____

Is there something God is putting on your heart to give? If yes, why do you think He wants you to give it? Keep in mind: you have resources outside of just money. God gives us time, finances, talents etc. as seed. What is it that you need, but that you have it in seed form?

_____

_____

_____

_____

_____

2) The world says that to be the greatest you need to work your way to the top. In the Kingdom, you become great by humbling yourself and being the least.

Read and Write down notes about Matthew 18:1-4

_____

_____

_____

_____

_____

Now, when you make yourself the "least", this is not instruction to allow yourself to be used and taken advantage of. Rather, when you are putting yourself in the "least" position, you are allowing God to work in your life in a great way! It is an example of being a servant. It is then HIS job to exalt you.

Read and Write Out Psalm 75:6

_____
_____
_____
_____
_____

What would promotion from the Lord look like in your personal life? What do you need to get there?

_____
_____
_____
_____
_____

3) The world demands that you fit into the way of the culture at any cost. The Kingdom is countercultural. What does that look like?

Read and Write Out Matthew 5:10-12, and discuss how it applies to the 3rd point.

_____
_____
_____
_____
_____

Living according to the laws of the Kingdom automatically puts us outside of the norm of any culture. It is not easy, but the promise of a greater reward than anything we could ever receive from the world helps us to remain focused on what God's purpose is and to see the struggles we face here on Earth from God's point of view. He has the big picture. Typically, we do not.

Read and Write Out Matthew 5:12

_____
_____
_____
_____
_____

What are some areas in your life or others' lives that you recognize differences between living according to the Kingdom and living according to what the world says?

_____
_____
_____
_____
_____

4) The world advises that you always look out for your own needs before the needs of others. In the Kingdom, you put others first before looking to your own needs.

Read and Write Out Matthew 20:16

_____

_____

_____

_____

Discuss: How is it applicable to putting others first?

Read and Write Out John 15:13

_____

_____

_____

_____

5) The world says to seek revenge for yourself. The Kingdom tells you to love your enemies and allow God to be their judge.

Read and Write Out Romans 12:19-20

_____

_____

_____

_____

Read and Write out Proverbs 20:22

_____

_____

_____

_____

*Discuss **Matthew 5:43-48***

Is there someone in your life who you need to give over to God and let Him handle?

_____

_____

_____

_____

_____

We can help guards our hearts from wanting to take revenge into our own hands by doing something God tells us a number of times in the Bible to do: FORGIVE.

Read and Write Out Matthew 6:12

_____

_____

_____

_____

If we want God to forgive us according to the same measure that we ask Him to forgive us, we should make sure we are forgiving others in the same way that we want to be forgiven by Him. Forgiveness means that whatever a person has done to you, you are letting whatever it was that was done be between them and God. IT IS NOT SAYING THT WHAT THEY DID WAS OK OR RIGHT!

IT IS saying that it is no longer your business. This can be a difficult concept to grasp because sometimes the measure of evil that was done to you can seem so great that it is hard to let go of. God knows this, and it takes His help to get you to be free from it. He loves you and the amount of freedom God can give over ANY situation is such a picture and example of His love for you.

Read and Write Out this promise from God found in Romans 8:28

_____

_____

_____

_____

Meditate on that verse. Imagine God taking all of the things that have happened to you and using them for your good.

Make a list of things that you still want to see flip and work for you. What does that look like? Is unforgiveness blocking God from being able to flip it? Are you ready to release it now?

What do you want to see "flipped" in your life?	Is there anything blocking you?

The principles of the Kingdom violate our natural way of thinking. Following them, however, brings a much greater reward than following the ways of the world.

ACT ON IT!

- Pray for other people for healing or a supernatural touch from God. Watch the kingdom come!
  Who are you praying for in these next two weeks? Write their names down and what you are praying for.

I'm praying for…	Their need is…

- How do you see your way of thinking changing as you start living by Kingdom laws rather than the "laws" of this world?

_____

_____

_____

_____

_____

The Kingdom

Week Three: Kingdom Happenings

When you enter the Kingdom and start modeling your life after the ways of the Kingdom you start to live supernaturally. As the Kingdom of Heaven comes to Earth, you begin to see elements of Heaven manifesting on Earth. The dead will be raised, because in the Kingdom, death does not exist. The sick will be healed, because in the Kingdom, people do not have to live with illness.

Read together out loud Matthew 10:7-8 and 1 Corinthians 4:20.

What are some of the ways we know the Kingdom of Heaven is near? Have you ever seen any of those ways in your life or others around you? Share with the group.

_____

_____

_____

_____

_____

What do the scriptures mean when they say that the Kingdom of God is not a matter of talk, but of power? Have you heard more talking during your Christian experience, or power? Why do you think that is? Discuss as a group.

1 Corinthians 4:20: "For the Kingdom of God is not a matter of talk but of power."

The Kingdom of Heaven is not some unreachable place.

Now that you know more about the Kingdom of God, the King's Domain, it's time to start speaking about it.

Part of manifesting the Kingdom is through your voice. It is by your words.

When you preach the good news of the Kingdom, you no longer have to live by certain natural laws. We live in a fallen world, and only through Jesus are curses able to be broken.

Read John 1.

As you spread Christ's message, the Kingdom inside of you pushes out into the earthly realm you live in. Then, the Kingdom becomes a complete lifestyle for you and others around you who accept the message.

Do you feel like, "Well that seems wonderful and all, but how come I haven't seen the Kingdom evident in my own life yet?"

The reason you haven't seen this in your life is because you haven't received it yet. Previously, you did not realize that you had access to the power of the Kingdom. The Kingdom is for you and is activated in your life now. You simply need to receive this in faith.

Read Romans 10:17

Where does this faith come from?

_____

_____

_____

_____

_____

Let's take a short detour and explore what this passage means. The Greek root of the word **'word'** given here in this passage is **rhema,** which means the spoken word of God.

Do you want more faith? Ask God to speak His word to you about the truth of Jesus Christ! God doesn't lie, and when you hear and receive the truth of the Gospel, faith comes.

Do you have faith? Do you believe the good news, the gospel of Jesus, that you have heard to be true? Have you ever heard the rhema word of God?

_____

_____

_____

_____

_____

You receive the Kingdom in order to give it away. Once you have it, go demonstrate the Kingdom for others!

ACT ON IT!

- Pray for other people for healing or a Supernatural encounter with God.
- Watch the Kingdom come! Who are you praying for in these next two weeks? Write their names down and what you are praying for.

I'm praying for…	Their need is…

- How do you see your way of thinking changing as you start living by the laws of the Kingdom?

_____
_____
_____
_____
_____

- How do you see Jesus manifesting the Kingdom, and what were some of the reactions He received?

_____
_____
_____
_____
_____

Realize that one of the biggest keys to manifesting the Kingdom is to learn more about the Kingdom. You do so by studying it out of His Word, and asking Him what that looks like. He's not afraid of your questions.

- In turn, you will be right in the middle of **Romans 12:1-2** and **Matthew 6:33**. Write those down here, and discuss the next time you meet with your group how they cooperate together.

Romans 12:1-2

_____
_____
_____
_____
_____

Matthew 6:33

_____
_____
_____
_____
_____

The Kingdom

Week Four: What Can Block the Kingdom?

As you enter the Kingdom, righteousness, peace, and joy will start to invade your life. The enemy, however, is going to want to block your access to the Kingdom, because in the Kingdom, Satan has no authority. Previously, you could not enter the Kingdom because of ignorance. You did not possess the knowledge of the Kingdom or your access to it. Now, Satan will employ different strategies to block your access to the Kingdom.

Read out loud together Romans 14:17

"For the Kingdom of God is not a matter of eating and drinking, but of righteousness, peace and joy in the Holy Spirit."

What can block the Kingdom? Natural Thinking. *What do you think Natural Thinking means?*

_____

_____

_____

_____

_____

When you think according to man's ways, your ability to enter the kingdom will be crippled. This happened to Peter when he did not elevate his mind in order to see the spiritual bird's eye view that God had when Jesus was arrested before His crucifixion. Read about it in the book of Matthew.

"From that time on Jesus began to explain to his disciples that he must go to Jerusalem and suffer many things at the hands of the elders, the chief priests and the teachers of the law, and that he must be killed and on the third day be raised to life. Peter took him aside and began to rebuke him. 'Never, Lord!' he said. 'This shall never happen to you!' Jesus turned and said to Peter, 'Get behind me, Satan! You are a stumbling block to me; you do not have in mind the concerns of God, but merely human concerns.'" Matthew 16:21-23

Jesus' thoughts were always in complete harmony with the Kingdom, and He understood that the opposite of God's ways were man's ways.

Take some time to recognize a current situation you are facing.

Write down in the circle on the left, your (natural) view of the situation. Then take time to pray about and ask what God's big picture of the situation is.

In the circle on the right, write down what God reveals to you. In the middle section, write down scripture that God is showing you to use to help you see the situation from His view and promises He has made to you.

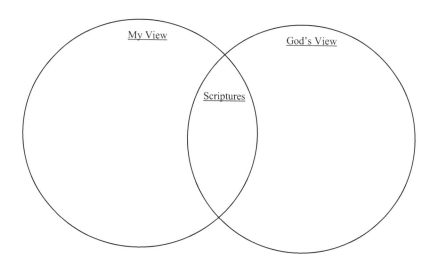

What can block the Kingdom? Fear. *What does this mean in your life? Are you fearful of anything? List your fears.*

_____

_____

_____

_____

_____

Read and Write Out Luke 12:32

_____
_____
_____
_____
_____

Read and Write Out 2 Timothy 1:7

_____
_____
_____
_____
_____

The recurring theme of the Kingdom is power! God wants us to work within the power of the Kingdom where there is no room for fear. Fear is a weapon the enemy will use to freeze you into your current state and prevent you from moving upward. God's love can pierce through fear and loosen you to enter the power of the Kingdom. Keep your focus on the love of God!

How can you fight these fears? Read **Ephesians 6:10-18**.

_____
_____
_____
_____
_____

What can block the Kingdom? Unbelief. *Is there a place in your life where unbelief exists? Why do you doubt?*

_____

_____

_____

_____

_____

Read the story in Mark 9:17-24.

Thoughts about this story:

_____

_____

_____

_____

_____

When the disciples could not drive out the demons, Jesus rebuked them for their unbelief. Believing in the ways of the Kingdom need to happen first before you bring the Kingdom to Earth. Jesus told them that everything is possible, and He meant absolutely **everything**. No matter how crazy you feel, believing that God can do anything is key for building up His Kingdom.

In what areas and specific situations has God already given you victories?

_____

_____

_____

_____

_____

What can block the Kingdom? Double-Mindedness. *Do you have this characteristic in your life?*

_____
_____
_____
_____
_____

Let's see what James has to say about double-mindedness.

Read and Write Out James 1:6-8

_____
_____
_____
_____
_____

When you ask the Lord to reveal the things of His Kingdom, plant your feet firmly in the ground with faith that the Lord will keep His promise of the Kingdom to you. No matter what you see happening in the natural realm around you, don't let it shake your stance. The Lord gives to the person **who** is not moved by outside circumstances.

ACT ON IT!

- What other things can you think of that are blocking you? Try to get specific.

_____

_____

_____

_____

_____

- Ask Jesus to give you a further revelation of the Kingdom. What is He showing you?

_____

_____

_____

_____

_____

Eve's Angels

Making the Tabernacle

Making the Tabernacle: Week One: Getting the Template

Everything in the Old Testament is a foreshadowing that may be applicable for us today. In the Old Testament, they built a place for God to live. In the New Testament, WE ARE the place where God lives. We are His tabernacle.

It says in Hebrews that we are the dwelling place of God. The truth is that God lives inside of you and has a very unique way He wants to design your life, your journey, and your story.

We can take what we learn from the Old Testament and see a foreshadowing of our lives today. The building of the tabernacle in Exodus is an example of that. Moses built a physical tabernacle in a very specific way. Since we are now the Tabernacle (or dwelling place) of the Holy Spirit, this applies to us now.

Write out the key points in Exodus 24:15-18

_____

_____

_____

_____

_____

How long did God wait to speak to Moses?

_____

The first thing Moses did was go up on the mountain, making time to spend alone with the Lord. God waited until Moses's seventh day there, which represents the day of rest, to speak.

Read Genesis 2:2

What does resting in God mean to you? How do you enter into that rest? How does what you believe about God affect your ability to rest?

_____
_____
_____
_____
_____

When Moses had finally entered a place of rest, having confidence that God would answer him, the Lord responded.

The Lord spends the next 14 chapters of the Bible explaining the details of His tabernacle. He made the instructions for the construction of the tabernacle very specific, and gave detailed directions for everything in the tabernacle, from the color of the curtains to the size of the altar.

In the same way, God has a specific blueprint stored in Heaven for your life. He is waiting for you to spend time in His perfect rest so He can answer when you ask Him what He wants your life to look like. His plans for you are intricately, perfectly, and beautifully designed.

Read and Write Out Jeremiah 29:11

_____
_____
_____
_____
_____

What do you believe about the plans God has for you? Do you have a vision or dream you are walking towards? Are you getting anything specific right now?

_____
_____
_____
_____
_____

Within this amazing design, it is important to note how God set up the tabernacle with an exact order for everything to be connected, allowing nothing to be haphazardly placed. Every part in the tabernacle is essential, even though not every part is connected.

The same applies to the body of Christ. Everything and everybody has a place, and sometimes that place is simply not in your life. If you tried to connect your foot to your head, you would not be able to walk. You can cause problems in the body if you are connecting yourself with the wrong people. This does not mean that they are wrong or unnecessary; you simply are not called to be connected to them. We are all still working towards the common goal of advancing God's Kingdom.

What kind of people, situations, or injustice are you called to invade? If you don't know specifically, sometimes your goals, talents, passions, and even the things that frustrate you can give hint to what arena this falls into. Jot them down here:

_____
_____
_____
_____
_____

How could your specific design be used to advance God's Kingdom right now?

_____
_____
_____
_____
_____

ACT ON IT!

- Take time this week and rest in God's presence. Stay in your quiet place until He speaks to you. It may be an impression, vision, dream or even a memory. His Word may bear witness in your spirit, or you may just have a sense of peace. Write it down and share the next time you meet.

_____

_____

_____

_____

_____

Making the Tabernacle

Week Two: A Life of Overflow

Once Moses relayed the instructions for the tabernacle to the Israelites, he took up an offering. The Israelites responded so enthusiastically to the truth of the template they gave much more than was needed for the construction. The offering was so plentiful Moses had to tell them to stop giving.

Read and write down anything that sticks out from Exodus 36: 4-7.

_____
_____
_____
_____
_____

When you are obedient to the Lord, structuring your life based off of the blueprint God has for you in Heaven, you will have more than enough.

You have to be in direct alignment with the pattern of Heaven, and then the abundance of Heaven will pour out on you. Jesus came to this Earth so we could live in this abundant life.

What would an abundant life look like to you?

_____

_____

_____

_____

_____

Read and Write Out John 10:10. Then read verse John 11

_____

_____

_____

_____

_____

The enemy tries his best to fool you into thinking that the riches of Heaven can never be for you. He wants to snatch your inheritance from you. With the knowledge that Jesus has gone before you so Heaven's blessings can be poured on you, you can claim what is rightfully yours through Christ. He came to give it to you, and even more than that.

Read and Write Out Malachi 3:10

_____

_____

_____

_____

_____

Read and Write Out Ephesians 3:20

_____
_____
_____
_____
_____

*What are you holding back from God, because you think
He is unable to answer?*

_____
_____
_____
_____
_____

The Lord's plan for you is way more than you can imagine,
and His blessings are endless. The key to unlocking the
fullness of the life He has for you is to completely replicate
the template of Heaven that God shows you for your life
specifically.

*If you are still struggling in any area, go back to God and
ask for new revelation about how your life was made to
look.*

Jesus is the perfect model of how to bring Heaven to earth. He is a complete reflection of God the Father, which is why He said, **"Anyone who has seen Me has seen the Father."**

Read John 14:9.

Jesus did not say or do anything without a revelation of Heaven from the Father. When Jesus imitated the Father, all of Heaven showed up as Jesus healed the sick, cast out demons, and performed miracles.

It is important to remember that God gave the directions one piece of furniture at a time, so don't get discouraged if He's not giving you the whole picture yet.

Follow what God has given you so far, trusting the next pieces of the picture will come at the exact time you need them.

If He does give you the whole picture, write it down and make choices for your life according to it. The pattern He gives you will help you to know what to do and say when making important decisions.

_____

_____

_____

_____

_____

ACT ON IT!

- Ask God to give you His Template. You will know that it is His Template when the resources show up supernaturally. Seek and you will find His promises.

- If you were to chart out the Blueprint for your life right now, what are some of the key points, people groups, or places you feel God is leading you towards?

Fill in the "Blueprints" for your life's mission:	What is God saying about this "blueprint" to you?
People Group:	
Places to Minister:	
Injustices to bring healing to:	
Creative Ideas to implement:	

Making the Tabernacle
Week Three: We ARE the Tabernacle

Read and Write Out the key points from 2 Peter 1:13-14

_____
_____
_____
_____
_____

From these verses, we understand that the earthly tabernacle is your *being*. We are the Tabernacle of the Lord and the Holy Spirit dwells in us, so we no longer need to look outside of ourselves to find the answers or to find God.

God can certainly use things outside of us as signs that point the way to Him, but the reflections of Him on the inside of you will ultimately be what point the way to the truth which is Jesus.

Have you had a person or sign from another place that pointed you towards God? When? REMEMBER: THERE ARE NO SUCH THINGS AS COINCIDENCES!!!

_____
_____
_____
_____

Have you ever had an impression from the Holy Spirit, dream, vision, word from the Lord bearing witness within you that pointed you towards God? When?

_____
_____
_____
_____
_____

Read and Write Out Exodus 25: 8-9

_____
_____
_____
_____
_____

God wanted to dwell among His people.

As you construct your lives in harmony with God's plan, you become His tabernacle.

God now dwells within YOU, His tabernacle. You ARE His tabernacle and He wants to dwell in you!

ACT ON IT!

- Spend some time this week just spending time with God. Dedicate time in your day where you have no other distractions.

- Focus on Jesus and Who He is in your life. Rest in His presence. BE with Him. Everything you DO is an extension of your BEING. As you BE with Him, your DOING will change. Don't try to do this in reverse order. It's just behavior modification, and true change never comes from this order. What you'll find is, as you spend time with Him, He will begin to show you who you ARE. FROM THAT PLACE....you DO.

Making the Tabernacle Week Four: Hope of Glory

What does, "Christ in you, the hope of glory", mean to you?

_____

_____

_____

_____

_____

Read and Write Out Colossians 1:27

_____

_____

_____

_____

_____

If Christ is in us, what does that change in your life right now?

_____

_____

_____

_____

_____

Read and Write Out Hebrews 8:10

_____
_____
_____
_____
_____

Look up the word "covenant" in the dictionary. What does covenant mean to you? Have you ever made a covenant with someone? Explain.

_____
_____
_____
_____
_____

When God gave Moses their laws, He wrote them on stone tablets to be placed in the tabernacle. Now that YOU are the tabernacle, He writes the laws and HIS WORD on your own heart and mind.

With God Himself residing in your being, you need the key to the answers He has placed in your heart. The key God gives you is the **Holy Spirit.**

Who is the Holy Spirit in your life?

_____

_____

_____

_____

_____

Look up the following scriptures about the Holy Spirit and fill in the blanks.

He is The Spirit of _____. Romans 8:9

He is The Spirit of _____. Genesis 1:2

He is the Spirit of our _____. Matthew 10:20

He is the Spirit of _____. John 14:17

He is the Spirit of _____. John 15:26

He is whom Christ sent to _____. John 16:7

What do you think the Holy Spirit's role in your life is?

_____

_____

_____

_____

_____

Read the following roles of the Holy Spirit out loud in your bible study group.

- **What is His Role?**

    o searches all things (1 Corinthians 2:10)

    o knows the mind of God (1 Corinthians 2:11)

    o teaches the content of the gospel to believers (1 Corinthians 2:13)

    o dwells among or within believers (1 Corinthians 3:16, Romans 8:11, 2 Timothy 1:14)

    o accomplishes all things (1 Corinthians 12:11)

    o gives life to those who believe (2 Corinthians 3:6)

    o cries out from within our hearts (Galatians 4:6)

    o leads us in the ways of God (Galatians 5:18, Romans 8:14)

    o bears witness with our own spirits (Romans 8:16)

    o has desires that are in opposition to the flesh (Galatians 5:17)

    o helps us in our WEAKNESS (Romans 8:26)

- intercedes on our behalf (Romans 8:26-27)

- works all things together for our ultimate good (Romans 8:28)

- strengthens believers (Ephesians 3:16)

- is grieved by our sinfulness (Ephesians 4:30)

- the fruit of the Spirit are the personal attributes of God (Galatians 5:22-23)

Read and Write Out Philippians 3:1-11

_____

_____

_____

_____

_____

What is the goal in life according to these scriptures?

_____

_____

_____

_____

_____

This is a brief introduction to the Spirit of God. I encourage you to get to know Him deeper and deeper.

ACT ON IT!

- Spend some time this week studying the scriptures on the Holy Spirit. If you have never talked to Him before, call on His name and invite His presence into your daily life. START NOW! There is nothing worth more than His presence.

- Write about something you learned about the Holy Spirit or from Him this week:

_____
_____
_____
_____
_____

Getting a Vision for Your Future

Week One: God Has a Plan for You

God wants to show you the spiritual truth of His will for your life. He has a plan, a template, and a reason why He does everything He does, including why He made you. Through relationship, He wants to show you what He created you for.

The very first thing He created was Light. Light causes us to see something, or know something new. It's our "ah ha" moment. God wants to give us that moment supernaturally. God is Spirit and He is Truth. There's no better place to function than out of your specific purpose. This world tells us that we're here to make money, go to school, work, and live a "normal" life. But when we became Christians, we traded our "normal" life for a Supernatural one.

Read and Write Out Jeremiah 29:11

_____

_____

_____

_____

_____

God knows the plans He has for you, and those plans are good! Trust that God is good and His plans for you are good. Trust that His plan is better than your plan. God is the manufacturer of your life. He made you and had something specific in mind when He did. It's time to ask the One Who made you what He had in mind.

God reveals His purpose in our life naturally and supernaturally. He has given us His Word, where He defines the life of a Christian, through the example of Christ.

The promises of God also help illustrate God's desire for our life. God clearly wrote His intentions for us in the Word.

God also reveals His plan for our lives through supernatural means such as dreams, visions, heavenly encounters, angelic visitations, words of wisdom, words of knowledge, and prophecy.

What have you discovered so far about God's plan, purpose, desire, and design for your life? Have people spoken words to you that you felt were true? Have you had dreams?

_____
_____
_____
_____
_____

What is your plan, purpose, will, desire, and design for your life?

_____

_____

_____

_____

_____

Let's look at some scriptures in the bible that speak about God's will for your life. Read the following scriptures, and write down anything that He speaks to you about these scriptures:

Romans 12:1-2

"Renew your Mind"

"Do not be conformed to this world, but be transformed by the renewal of your mind, that by testing you may discern what is the will of God, what is good and acceptable and perfect."

_____

_____

Romans 15:30

"Pray for Your Brothers"

"I appeal to you, brothers, by our Lord Jesus Christ and by the love of the Spirit, to strive together with me in your prayers to God on my behalf."

_____

_____

Hebrews 10: 35-36

"Be Confident in Endurance"

"Therefore do not throw away your confidence, which has a great reward. For you have need of endurance, so that when you have done the will of God you may receive what is promised."

_____

_____

Isaiah 30:21

"Hear His Voice"

"And your ears will hear a word behind you, "This is the way, walk in it," whenever you turn to the right or to the left."

_____

_____

Philippians 2:13

"Let Him Use You"

"For it is God who is at work in you, both to will and to work for His good pleasure."

_____

_____

Proverbs 3:5-6

"Trust Him"

"Trust in the LORD with all your heart, And do not lean on your own understanding. In all your ways acknowledge Him, And He will make your paths straight."

_____

_____

Psalm 37: 4

"Delight Yourself"

"Delight yourself in the Lord and He will give you the desires of your heart."

_____

_____

1 Thessalonians 5:18

"Give Thanks"

"In everything give thanks: for this is the will of God in Christ Jesus concerning you."

_____

_____

2 Corinthians 5:17

"Receive Your New Identity"

"Therefore if any man be in Christ, he is a new creature: old things are passed away; behold, all things are become new."

_____

_____

ACT ON IT!

- Go back to the inquiry questions and add some more reflection based on what we studied this lesson.
- What is one area in your life that you will specifically pray about this week for God to intervene and establish His perfect will?

_____

_____

_____

_____

_____

Getting a Vision for Your Future
Week Two: The Vision

Read the following key scriptures together in your group.

Proverbs 29:18: "Where there is no vision, the people perish: but he that keepeth the law, happy is he."

Deuteronomy 29:29: "The secret things belong to the LORD our God, but the things that are revealed belong to us and to our children forever, that we may do all the words of this law."

Psalm 139:16: "Your eyes saw my unformed substance; in your book were written, every one of them, the days that were formed for me, when as yet there was none of them."

What did you want to be when you were little? Sometimes our purest thoughts give hint to our destiny.

_____

_____

_____

_____

_____

If there was no such thing as money, what would you do? What would your day consist of? Seek God for your purpose. Pray into purpose.

_____
_____
_____
_____
_____

What lies can you identify that have stopped you from becoming who you want to be? i.e. not smart enough...

_____
_____
_____
_____
_____

Write down the following scriptures together in your group.

1 Corinthians 14:1

_____
_____
_____
_____
_____

John 16:13

_____

_____

_____

_____

_____

These are two promises that you can stand on. If Jesus said the word, then both of these things are true. Pray for the Spirit of Truth to give you a new way of thinking so you can know what His good and acceptable will is.

EXPAND YOUR VISION!

Recall: **Romans 12:2 "Do not be conformed to this world, but be transformed by the renewal of your mind, that by testing you may discern what is the will of God, what is good and acceptable and perfect."**

In order to get the will and purpose of God, you have to have your mind renewed. If you're struggling, it's because you're thinking with your natural mind, and the natural mind is at enmity with the mind of the spirit.

Read Romans 8:7 "For the mind that is set on the flesh is hostile to God, for it does not submit to God's law; indeed, it cannot."

You're not going to be able to figure this out. You're going to need a revelation because the will of God for your life is more than you can imagine!

Read Ephesians 3:20 "Now to Him who is able to do far more abundantly than all that we ask or think, according to the power at work within us."

His Plans for you are bigger than you can even imagine.

If your current vision seems possible, then you're thinking too small. What does God's Word have to say about this?

Read Isaiah 54:2

"Enlarge the place of your tent, and let the curtains of your habitations be stretched out; do not hold back; lengthen your cords and strengthen your stakes."

Read Matthew 19:26

"But Jesus looked at them and said, "With man this is impossible, but with God all things are possible."

Are there any plans you can ditch right now because you are recognizing that God's moving you into a more impossible path to accomplish with Him?

_____

_____

_____

_____

_____

ACT ON IT!

- Spend time praying on your own and ask the Lord to show you something. Sit quietly and wait for His voice. Pay attention to the different ways He might be speaking to you. It could be through a vision, a smell, a sound, song lyrics that come into your mind, anything. Keep your heart open with expectation.

_____

_____

_____

_____

_____

Getting a Vision for Your Future

Week Three: Be Persistent

Haven't gotten an answer on your purpose yet? Keep pressing in.

Pray **Ephesians 1: 18:20** over the group before you start bible study tonight.

"I pray that the eyes of your heart may be enlightened in order that you may know the hope to which He has called you, the riches of His glorious inheritance in His holy people, and His incomparably great power for us who believe He exerted when He raised Christ from the dead and seated Him at His right hand in the heavenly realms." (NIV)

In another translation, **"I pray that the eyes of your heart may be enlightened, so that you will know what is the hope of His calling, what are the riches of the glory of His inheritance in the saints, and what is the surpassing greatness of His power toward us who believe. These are in accordance with the working of the strength of His might which He brought about in Christ, when He raised Him from the dead and seated Him at His right hand in the heavenly places." (NASB)**

What is this scripture revealing to us about God's power and purpose?

_____

_____

_____

_____

_____

Basically, your heart will *see* your purpose. You can stand on these words.

Read this story in Luke 11: 5-13:

"Then, teaching them more about prayer, he used this story: "Suppose you went to a friend's house at midnight, wanting to borrow three loaves of bread. You say to him, 'A friend of mine has just arrived for a visit, and I have nothing for him to eat.' And suppose he calls out from his bedroom, 'Don't bother me. The door is locked for the night, and my family and I are all in bed. I can't help you.' But I tell you this—though he won't do it for friendship's sake, if you keep knocking long enough, he will get up and give you whatever you need because of your shameless persistence. And so I tell you, keep on asking, and you will receive what you ask for. Keep on seeking, and you will find. Keep on knocking, and the door will be opened to you. For everyone who asks, receives. Everyone who seeks, finds. And to everyone who knocks, the door will be opened. You fathers—if your children ask for a fish, do you give them a snake instead? Or if they ask for an egg, do you

give them a scorpion? Of course not! So if you sinful people know how to give good gifts to your children, how much more will your heavenly Father give the Holy Spirit to those who ask Him?"

What is God saying in this scripture about the type of Father He is?

_____

_____

_____

_____

_____

Sometimes when we ask God for things, we don't hear from Him right away. That doesn't mean He's ignoring us. God wants to reveal His will to you. If you believe and have faith in this, He will show it to you.

Read the parable in Luke 18:1-8

"And He told them a parable to the effect that they ought always to pray and not lose heart. He said, "In a certain city there was a judge who neither feared God nor respected man. And there was a widow in that city who kept coming to him and saying, 'Give me justice against my adversary.' For a while he refused, but afterward he said to himself, 'Though I neither fear God nor respect man, yet because this widow keeps bothering me, I will give her justice, so that she will not beat me down by her continual coming.' And the Lord said, "Hear what the unrighteous judge says. And will not God give justice to his elect, who cry to Him day and night? Will he delay long over them? I tell you, He will give justice to them speedily. Nevertheless, when the

Son of Man comes, will He find faith on earth?"

Be persistent, the Lord is faithful. He can't deny Himself. Take heart for He will not delay, but come speedily.

ACT ON IT!

- If you haven't heard what your purpose is, or had an 'ah ha' moment, what could you do to press in to get it?

_____

_____

_____

_____

_____

- Look for repetitive patterns or coincidences. The Spirit of Truth will speak to you this week. Ask God to open up your eyes to see and your ears to hear. He could speak to you through a number, a repeated theme, a person, a picture, a song, etc. Look for something that comes up over and over again. Ask God to specifically show you. Specific prayers get specific answers! Make sure you remove all feelings of unworthiness. Know your identity as the Bride of Christ.

- Write down the patterns, repetitions, and coincidences here:

Patterns	
Repetitions	
Coincidences	

- Memorize this scripture:
  Hebrews 4:16 "Let us then with confidence draw near to the throne of grace, that we may receive mercy and find grace to help in time of need."

Getting a Vision for Your Future

Week Four: Share the Vision

This week we want you to go around and share the vision God has been giving you. Encourage one another as each person shares. Call out the gifts in others that you see. Pray for each person in the group.

Find the following scriptures and read together in your group.

- **Habakkuk 2:2**
- **Psalms 37:23**
- **Luke 16:10**
- **2 Corinthians 3:18**

Write Out Habakkuk 2:2

_____
_____
_____
_____
_____

What did the Lord tell Habakkuk to do with his vision? How are we able to help others get empowered by the vision God is sharing with us?

_____
_____
_____
_____
_____

When you write it down on paper, you're able to run with it and others can start where you left off. You can put it into action more effectively.

Write Out Psalms 37:23

_____
_____
_____
_____
_____

Look back at your life before you began to know the Lord and have a relationship with Him. Where do you see God leading your steps during that season?

_____
_____
_____
_____
_____

Think about your life now that you have been choosing to grow your relationship with God. Where do you see the Lord establishing your steps?

_____
_____
_____
_____
_____

God may only give you one step at a time. You may be wondering what's next. Sometimes, He only shows you one step. In order to reach the fulfillment of His vision for you, you have to do the first thing He showed you.

Write Out Luke 16:10

_____
_____
_____
_____
_____

What has He given you that you can grow and expand?

_____
_____
_____
_____
_____

Even if you only see a little bit of it now, keep following the light.

Write Out 2 Corinthians 3:18

_____
_____
_____
_____
_____

Pray for each other after sharing your visions.

<u>ACT ON IT!</u>

- Write down what He's shown you so far, even if it's just a list of clues. There's no such thing as coincidences. Write those down too.

_____
_____
_____
_____
_____

- Share what you've heard from the Lord so far with a family member or a close friend.

- What was their reaction? Did it make sense to them in light of knowing you? Sometimes, the thing He's calling us to is more obvious to others than it is to ourselves.

_____
_____
_____
_____
_____

- What is one practical step that you can take right now to put the vision into practice?

_____
_____
_____
_____
_____

Healing Your Heart

Week One: Guard Your Heart

Jesus came to make a new order. His goal is to bring the Kingdom of Heaven to Earth. Since we are followers of Him that's exactly what we are supposed to be doing. However, we cannot do that if we are not functioning correctly. The most common malfunction in people today is the broken heart. Having a broken heart can affect your breakthrough.

Read and Write Out Matthew 12:34

_____

_____

_____

_____

_____

Since we are like Jesus, we birth the Kingdom through our words. When God created, He spoke. We are made in His Image. We advance His Realm by the words that we say, and by having the Truth inside of your heart, you create His Realm. We are kings, and He is the King of us. We are lords, and He is our Lord. Lining up your words, not just with your mouth but with your heart is key. It changes things. It influences things. It brings Heaven to Earth.

Read and Write Out Psalm 103:20

_____
_____
_____
_____
_____

When you speak the words He's put in your heart, Angels harken to it. They move because of it. They recognize the frequency as being truth, and they move. You move Heaven by lining up with it. It's hard to carry that truth with a broken heart.

There are many ways for us to get our hearts broken. Since we are in the flesh we think in the flesh and allow the ways of this world to affect us.

Your heart may be broken by soul trauma, a loved one disappointed you, deception, pain, hurt, or humiliation. When you don't let God in to heal your broken situation, you will fall victim to a whole mess of things that will only make the situation worse.

An unhealed heart leads to bitterness, anger, and fear. All of these inhibit your ability to bring the Kingdom, which is your purpose. So, if the enemy can strike fear into your heart, or cause a situation that hurts you in your walk, and you don't heal from that initial heartbreak, he is keeping you from your purpose.

What do your words and what you talk about the most reveal about your heart?

_____

_____

_____

_____

_____

How has your heart been broken?

_____

_____

_____

_____

_____

Faith is held in your heart. If your heart is broken, you can't carry the substance promised to you.

Read and Write Out Luke 17:5-6

_____

_____

_____

_____

_____

Do you understand that at your full potential, through your faith in Christ, you have the power to command and rule? There is a spiritual war over our faith. It will always boil down to your relationship with Jesus. Imagine your heart is a cup that God pours into.

If you have a hole in the cup halfway down, you can only carry half of what is yours because the cup would leak.

However, God desires that your cup (your heart) be without holes, so that He can fill you and what He pours into you can overflow onto others.

Read and Write Out Psalm 34:18

_____
_____
_____
_____
_____

Read and Write Out Psalm 147:3

_____
_____
_____
_____
_____

When we are brokenhearted and cry out to God, He is there; He draws near. You know the type of prayer I'm talking about; the on your face, snot dripping down your chin, not caring who hears kind of prayer.

The kind of cry out to God that reveals you know He is the only way out of the situation you're in, no matter how you got into it. He wants us to be at the end of ourselves so that He can come in and do what He does best: bind everything up.

What holes do you have in your cup right now? How did they get there, and will you allow them to be healed?

_____

_____

_____

_____

_____

Guarding our hearts is one of the most important things we can do to prevent from getting holes in the first place. If our cups are firmly planted in truth they are impermeable from the outside in, there is no way for people and situations to cause a leak.

How do you guard your heart? Stay firmly planted in the truth. If you know where your identity is rooted and in Whom it is anchored with, there is no way anything can break through.

As we discussed in the previous chapter, the truth is Jesus.

Read John 14:6

"Jesus answered, 'I am the way and the truth and the life. No one comes to the Father except through me.'"

So, if He is the truth, then we need to seek Him in His Word. Knowing what He is saying, and believing it above anything else is the weapon to use while guarding your heart.

Part of the redemptive work of Christ is filling in the holes in our broken hearts. Let's be honest, apart from Jesus Christ, we all suffer from broken hearts. Because of what He did on the cross, you are to be filled until it spills over onto everyone around you. You can't lose. So let God come in and fix those parts of your heart that are broken.

Read and Write Out John 10:10

_____

_____

_____

_____

_____

Read 1 Timothy 6:12

"Fight the good fight of faith."

Clearly, Satan is after something. The thing he's after is your faith. The way he takes it is by breaking the container in which it's held in. The good news is, no matter what the enemy has been able to do up until this point, God gave us Jesus which is the answer to the broken heart.

Read and Write Out Luke 4:18

_____

_____

_____

_____

_____

Read Isaiah 53:5

"But he was pierced for our transgressions; he was crushed for our iniquities; upon him was the chastisement that brought us peace, and with his wounds we are healed."

ACT ON IT!

- Identify three places where your heart is broken (any hurt, disappointment, etc.) that you want God to mend. Next to each one, ask yourself what is blocking your healing. Ask God to take over the healing process for those hurtful areas in your life. You may not know what this looks like, but He does. Give it to Him.

Places Where Your Heart Needs Healing:	What is blocking that healing from taking place?
1.	
2.	
3.	

Pray that God would reveal certain things to you about how to be mended from your broken heart.

- Memorize **Psalms 34:18 which says, "The LORD is near to the brokenhearted and saves the crushed in spirit."**

Healing Your Heart

Week Two: Anointing Comes From Pressure

"The Spirit of the Lord is on me,
because he has anointed me
to proclaim good news to the poor.
He has sent me to proclaim freedom for the prisoners
and recovery of sight for the blind,
to set the oppressed free" Luke 4:18

Anything that God delivers you from, gives you the capacity to set others free in that area. He has brought you through the test giving you a testimony. After you've been broken in a certain area, and God comes along and heals your heart, you can go and minister to others.

Read Isaiah 35:3-4

"**Strengthen the weak hands, and make firm the feeble knees. Say to those who have an anxious heart, "Be strong; fear not! Behold, your God will come with vengeance, with the recompense of God. He will come and save you."**

Have you been healed from a broken heart? In the space below write what happened that required the healing and how God did that for you. If not, how do you plan to continue to seek God's healing for what has been broken?

_____
_____
_____
_____
_____

We are to take our healing and go encourage someone else with it. We need to bring other women a message of joy, hope and love because we know from our own life's experiences that God will come through. God will heal them.

Read and Write Out Psalm 107:20

_____
_____
_____
_____
_____

He sends out His Word through YOU!!!!

There is power in His word, we must go and take the word we were given- that healed us- and go give that to someone else.

Who in your life can you go share this message with? What is holding you back?

_____

_____

_____

_____

_____

If our purpose is to bring the Kingdom of Heaven here to Earth, and we are just becoming aware of this now, are there others still unaware?

Read and Write Out Luke 17:20-21

_____

_____

_____

_____

_____

Read and Write Out Luke 24:45

_____

_____

_____

_____

_____

God loves you so much that He sent His only Son, Jesus, as a sacrifice to bring the Kingdom. His Kingdom is in you.

When He died on the cross the spiritual battle was won. Jesus came to bring His Kingdom in you and through you so that others may see that we now have victory in Him.

He opens your mind to truth, and you are now a witness to these things, so you may be a witness to others. It is through the things He shows you that you're to go show others. This is Kingdom Expansion. This comes from being able to believe His Truth. Believing comes from the heart.

Read and Write Out Revelation 12:11

_____
_____
_____
_____
_____

Read Revelation 19:10

"For the testimony of Jesus is the spirit of prophecy."

The testimony that Jesus has done in your life is the spirit of prophecy. The spirit of prophecy means, it has the ability, when you tell it, to make itself come to pass again. When you tell someone what He has done in your life, the Spirit of God is given permission to do it again in that person's life. **Has He healed your heart? TELL IT!!!**

In the space below, write out a one minute version of your testimony. What has God brought you through, and how can you personally share the good news with others? You want to be ready for when the opportunity arises.

_____
_____
_____
_____
_____
_____
_____
_____
_____

ACT ON IT!

- Think about places in your life that God has healed.

- Pick two people to share your testimony with. Are there any that you are confident would be a blessing to someone else who happens to be going through the same thing you were going through? Who are they and what happened?

Who are the two people?	What happened?
1.	
2.	

Healing Your Heart

Week Three: Fight the Good Fight of Faith

The war is over what you believe. The devil will try everything to distort your perception and aide you in believing a lie. It's easier to believe what God is telling you when your heart is mended. After you are done mending, continue to fight for yourself and for others!

Read and Write Out Proverbs 3:5-6

_____

_____

_____

_____

_____

We need to guard our hearts from the wrong perspective. **Proverbs 4:23** says, **"Guard your heart with all diligence for it is the wellspring of life."**

We all have a tendency to fall back into the flesh's way of "practical" thinking. When we doubt what God can do, we are imitating brokenness; we are leaning on our own understanding. Faith comes by hearing the spoken word of God. Fighting with that faith changes things. Faith is the currency of heaven.

Read the story of Jesus and Lazarus in **John 11**.

When Jesus wept and groaned, it was not because of sadness, or loss. Jesus says that death will not come of this, but rather it has happened so that God would be glorified, but no one believed Him. His sadness was in their lack of faith, in their broken hearts, and in their hopelessness.

What is an impossible situation or person in your life right now?

_____

_____

_____

_____

_____

When Lazarus does die, and Jesus tells Martha that he will live again, He meant literally. She thought He meant in the Resurrection.

Jesus' response was that He WAS the resurrection. It was by His power that Lazarus would be raised. Martha had to believe that for herself. She had to have faith, but it was hard because her heart was broken.

Faith comes by hearing the spoken word of God. The words that Jesus spoke were the spoken word of God. **Read John 12:49.**

Jesus had faith. He knew what He could do, and so Lazarus was healed.

This principle is demonstrated many times in the Bible. When Jesus traveled and healed people, He often did so and remarked at the fact that those people had faith, they believed.

Read Luke 8:40-56

The woman with the issue of blood had enough faith to just reach out and touch Him. She knew that if she could just do that, she would be healed. Her cup was full, like we learned about in week one.   Jairus had faith for his daughter, when he came to Jesus he said that he knew He could heal her. His cup was full.

Read Matthew 8:5-13

When the Roman centurion, a gentile, came to Jesus because one of his men was sick he said that he knew all Jesus had to do was say the word, and this man would be healed. His cup was full. When our broken hearts are healed, we need to have full cups. Our faith in who God is, what He can do and will do, is what we bring to other people so that Jesus can heal their hearts as well.

In some of these stories, it was other people going to Jesus on behalf of the sick, or dead, or wounded. Your faith can affect other people who are battling with the lies of the enemy. You can fight on their behalf.

When things get tough you can do one of two things; either what you see in front of you becomes your reality, or you believe in what God told you. The enemy has been setting you up from birth to have cracks in your heart, so that when God comes, you will leak. However, God means what He says!

Read and Write Out John 10:10

_____

_____

_____

_____

_____

The enemy shows up when you just got the word or you have a word from God that is coming. The real fight is not what you see. The fight is over what reality you will accept.

Read and Write Out 2 Corinthians 5:7

_____

_____

_____

_____

_____

Take a minute to reflect: What reality do you believe? What do your actions show?

_____

_____

_____

_____

_____

What promises, that God has given you, are you struggling to have faith in? What is blocking your belief that God will come through?

_____
_____
_____
_____
_____

ACT ON IT!

- Find ways to fight what you see with what God told you by finding truth to combat "your own understanding." Make a list of things you are lacking faith in. The Index of your Bible has a list of topics. Go through it and find scripture to reveal truth on those topics.

List the topics that you are lacking faith in here:	Write down scripture to reveal truth about these topics here:
1.	
2.	
3.	
4.	

Healing Your Heart

Week Four: Revival

Prophetic ministry, for the unbeliever, is giving them an encounter with the Holy Spirit. We are called to bring the Kingdom of Heaven to other people. When we have been filled up with God's love, we can go and pour love into the lives of others.

Revival starts with Jesus. Revival begins when you remember who you are in Him. We can remind people of this to start revival in places and in people that have been lost in darkness. We can bring the light to them. We have to be ready for them; we need to have faith for them; healing for them; faith to move the mountains for them; have faith that binds their broken hearts.

We know that **Matthew 11:23** says, **"Truly I tell you, if you have faith and do not doubt, not only can you do what was done to the fig tree, but also you can say to this mountain, 'Go, throw yourself into the sea,' and it will be done."**

We have to live like we know what **Matthew 11:23** says.

What would revival look like in your life?

_____

_____

_____

_____

_____

Look up the word REVIVAL in a dictionary. Write down anything that speaks to you specifically.

_____

_____

_____

_____

_____

There is going to be a harvest that we have to get ready for. Our salvation, our revelations, and our gifts were not given to us for our own personal amusement!

The whole point of being filled by the Spirit is so that we can be poured out again into someone else's life. So, why aren't we pouring out?!

We shouldn't be like small buckets outside collecting raindrops, as if that's the only water we will get. We should never have to go thirsty!

We have access to an unending river of life, so we can pour and pour and pour and always continue to be filled! God allows us to take part in bringing His Kingdom!

Rivers FLOW. A river is what carved out the Grand Canyon. That is what you have access to flowing out of your spiritual belly, giving birth to spiritual things. You are a force to be reckoned with.

Who in your life are you pouring into? Who is pouring into you?

_____

_____

_____

_____

_____

Read Revelation 22

Write out some thoughts about God's River of Life.

_____

_____

_____

_____

_____

<u>ACT ON IT!</u>

- Think back to those places we dealt with in week one of this section. Write about how God has provided healing in those areas so far.

_____

_____

_____

_____

_____

- Pray and ask God to bring and show you people who are broken in the same way, and show them the Kingdom. Praise God for what He has brought you through.

Breaking Through Impossibility

Week One: Nothing is Impossible

When you are in the Kingdom, you are playing by God's rules. One of God's rules says that there is no such thing as "impossible". This seems like a simple statement at first glance. However, when fully understood, the results can be terrifying to the devil.

Read together the story of Sarah in Genesis 18:1-14.

What did God do for Sarah? Discuss as a group why this was so important to a woman living in that time?

_____
_____
_____
_____
_____

God gave a promise to Abraham and Sarah to provide a son, who would in turn fulfill God's promise of making Abraham the Father of all nations. Women in that time put a lot of weight of their worth into the heir they produced for their husband. It was seen as the woman's fault if she could not bear children, as if something must be wrong with her physically or spiritually.

God spoke to Abraham and Sarah and told them that they were to have a child, even in their old age! At this point in the game, having a baby was physically impossible for them. They were too old.

Their time should have been up. You may feel that it is too late for you to see the fullness of God's promises come to pass in your own life, but clearly, as this story in scripture demonstrates, it's never too late.

Read and Write Out Genesis 18:1

_____
_____
_____
_____
_____

When God shows up, everything changes.

Has God ever shown you something that originally seemed impossible, but as your perspective changed, it became a reality? Has He ever spoken to you through someone else or an impression that changed a circumstance you were facing?

_____
_____
_____
_____
_____

Abraham was sitting around like it was any other day. He was running camp, taking care of his responsibilities. He was just sitting down to rest when the three unexpected strangers came and rocked his world.

When God comes through it may be a surprise to you, but it is no surprise to God. He comes in the midst of our busy schedules. He may even show up when you think you may not be ready.

Abraham was not on his knees praying when the men arrived, he was not building an altar to atone for his sins, he was sitting and resting. I love that! It is never about what we are DOING that interests God, because He sees our hearts! He wants us to spread His name throughout the Earth and so He uses extraordinary events to do so sometimes.

You don't need to be anyone or be doing anything extraordinary in order for God to use you because you already ARE someone, and have the capacity to do extraordinary things. You just don't know it yet.

Is there anything in your life that you regret not doing, or do you feel like some things have just passed you by?

_____

_____

_____

_____

_____

Satan wants to keep you in a world where you believe things just won't happen for you. If he can keep your ideas of what God can do small, then you give him a large part of control in the game, which really is no game at all, it's your eternity.

ACT ON IT!

- Identify those things you feel are too late for you. Take the time to write down those desires and ask the Lord if any of them are still the desires He has for your life. What is He showing you?

_____
_____
_____
_____
_____
_____

- **Memorize Genesis 18:14** Speak it out loud to yourself when doubt starts to creep in. It will change your life.

Breaking Through Impossibility

Week Two: God's Strength

Read and Write Out Isaiah 50:2

_____
_____
_____
_____
_____

We see God's answer to the Israelites' complaining. They were the chosen people of God and yet had assumed that God had left them in their despair, since they were suffering and bad things were happening to them.

Can you think of a time when you felt like God had abandoned you in your suffering?

_____
_____
_____
_____
_____

Situations may arise that seem impossible to get out of. They can be financial, physical, emotional, etc. It appears like the wheels on the bus keep going round and round with no exit in sight.

You can't imagine change even as an option, so you've almost grown accustomed to the frustrations of your situation. Sometimes to see circumstances start to turn, it's as easy as asking God to remove it.

Read and Write Out James 4:2

_____
_____
_____
_____
_____

God can do "suddenlys" and miracles! In, fact, He is very good at them. The Bible is full of them. Right when God's people had grown so weary, and they didn't know how much more they could take, BOOM! God shows up and switches everything around. Guess what?

Read and Write Out Hebrews 13:8

_____
_____
_____
_____
_____

God's ability to intervene in hopeless circumstances has not expired. If He did it for His people then, He will do it for you now.

Sometimes to see circumstances start to turn, it's as easy as asking God to turn it.

God wants to come through for us. In order for that to happen we need to first ask, and when He comes through, we need to be there to listen.

What situations in your life have you simply grown accustomed to, that you know God wants to free you from?

_____

_____

_____

_____

_____

Read and Write Out Jeremiah 32:17

_____

_____

_____

_____

_____

Take a moment to think about this truth, the Lord has made all the Heavens and the Earth, nothing is too hard for Him.

He made the entire universe! Don't think of this fact as a theory, but a reality. It will flip your faith and strengthen it. God is so much bigger than the box we so often put him in.

We shape Him into our own image, we shape Him into being like the people around us who claim to know Him, and we even compare our experience with God to that which we have with other people.

Let's start on a clean slate with our Creator. He is not like anything we have ever seen or known. His grace and power is infinite!

ACT ON IT!

- Make a list of things that would require the strength of God on your behalf to change the course of your life. Make both a short term list and a long term list. Keep this list on you throughout the week (in your wallet, purse, or pocket), and continue to talk to God about it. God will intervene!

Short Term List
1.
2.
3.
4.

Long Term List
1.
2.
3.
4.

Breaking Through Impossibility:

Week Three: God Has No Limits

Read and Write Out Jeremiah 32:26-27

_____
_____
_____
_____
_____

TIME TO TAKE THE LIMITS OFF OF GOD!

Time after time, we see God doing what is obviously not possible for us to do. Yet He uses us to do it. This question He asks of His people in Jeremiah is not to be answered. It is rhetorical, so it answers itself.

We see the Lord asking rhetorical questions often to bring us into agreement with His Truth.

Jeremiah knew that nothing was too hard for God. But it was necessary for him to hear that truth at that time. It reminded him of the truth, regardless of the mess he was going through. It erased his doubt.

God wants to reveal truth individually to us even though we may have our doubts.

Read and Write Out Psalm 37:7

_____

_____

_____

_____

_____

Our God is able, and over all mankind. Absolutely nothing is too hard for Him to accomplish in your life!

How does that encourage you with the decisions and opportunities you may have today?

_____

_____

_____

_____

_____

We are told to be still before the Lord and to wait patiently for Him. If we are trying to fix things our own way, God will in turn patiently wait for us to stop struggling and realize He is the only way.

Read and Write Out 2 Peter 3:9

_____
_____
_____
_____
_____

God is completely self-sufficient. Nothing is beyond His reach or ability. He has no limits on what He can to do in your life, through your life, and with your life.

Read Jeremiah 32: 26-27

Now take this statement He is making and combine it with **Romans 8:28.**

Read and Write Out Romans 8:28

_____
_____
_____
_____
_____

These truths combined provide serious revelation that can knock down the walls of any limit in your life.

What is it that you think can separate you from God's love and provision?

What if God could take everything that the enemy meant for evil in your past, and somehow use it for your good? What would that look like? Again, when thinking through this question, don't limit God. Go through your past with a fine-toothed comb. Bring even the smallest setbacks to God and ask Him how He can redeem it.

Romans 8:38-39 says, "For I am convinced that neither death nor life, neither angels nor demons, neither the present nor the future, nor any powers, neither height nor depth, nor anything else in all creation, will be able to separate us from the love of God that is in Christ Jesus our Lord."

What if you could become fully persuaded that the God of the Universe knew you before you ever got here? He knew what you would be going through right now. He had in all of His infinite wisdom, an escape plan, a plan of restoration, and a plan of revival for your life.

We are talking about the type of plan that can flip the whole script of your life so that no matter if you were to blame for your struggles or not, you can then use them as a stepping stone right into your destiny.

It's His promise. God's word is true so, His promises are true.

Does God want to redeem absolutely everything? Yes! Take that to heart, and in the space below spend time asking Him to redeem specific things in your life that Satan meant for your destruction.

_____

_____

_____

_____

_____

ACT ON IT!

- Take the plans you have now, and play the "What-if?" game with God. What if God did this? What if God showed up and took control of this particular area of my life? Take the worst thing that ever happened in your life and ask God to work it for your good. Talk to a close friend about what this would look like. BELIEVE GOD FOR THE BIG!

"WHAT IF" God did...	Imagine the outcome:
1.	
2.	
3.	
4.	
5.	
6.	

Breaking Through Impossibility

Week Four: Surrender

These are some definitions when asking people what they think SURRENDER means:

a. to give power, control, or possession of to another when they demand it

b. to give up completely or agree especially in favor of another

c: to give yourself up into the power as if you are a prisoner

d: to give yourself over to something by giving them influence over you

What things in your life, according to the above definitions, have you been surrendering to?

_____
_____
_____
_____
_____

Read Luke 18:18-27

Jesus points out that impossibility, when left up to humans, is still impossibility. Too many times, we take our problems and feel like we need to fix them. This is what we call "works mode".

When we think that we have to be the solution to our problem, whatever "solution" we find will always fall short of what God wanted to do.

Sometimes the answer is to surrender the problem to God because we were never meant to fix it in the first place.

Read and Write Out Matthew 19:26

_____
_____
_____
_____
_____

The path God leads us down, whether there are trials or not, is usually meant to show us more of Himself.

Recognizing that He is the giver of all things and through Him anything can come to pass is the first step towards believing in God all things are possible.

What are some of the paths God has led you down, or is currently leading you down? What is it that you think He may be showing you through this?

_____
_____
_____
_____
_____

What is a situation you can't let go of because you don't think God will be there to catch it when you do?

_____
_____
_____
_____
_____

Read and Write Out John 14:6

_____
_____
_____
_____
_____

He doesn't just tell you the truth. He IS the truth.

There was once a group of hikers winding the trails of Columbia following a guide who knew the paths like the back of his hand. The hikers were getting weary from the heat, distance, and the mosquito's biting at their ankles.

One of the hikers towards the back yelled up to the guide, "Guide, I need to stop! Please point out on my map the path I should take so I can meet up with you in a little while?" The guide stopped, walked back towards the man and said "That is not possible; I cannot show you the path, for I AM the path you seek." The guide then handed the man a canteen of water and some bug spray knowing he needed rest.

Sometimes we are too busy thinking about the next steps we need to take, relying on our own strength, that we miss the answer directly in front of us.

Jesus, the Son of God, is our Guide. He is the way to peace, everlasting life, redemption, and sanctification. **Our maps are of no use. He is what we seek.** You desire rest? Ask your Guide. You desire peace? Ask your Guide. You want to see an impossible situation made possible? Ask your Guide. He will give you things you didn't even know you needed.

Read 2 Corinthians 12:10

"My grace is sufficient for you, for my power is made perfect in weakness. Therefore I will boast all the more gladly about my weaknesses, so that Christ's power may rest on me."

Go to Him in truth and transparency. Tell Him exactly what is on your heart. However you really see your situation, as bleak as it may be, as weak as you may feel, talk to Him about it and He will give you His perspective.

What prevents you from talking to God like this, honestly?

_____

_____

_____

_____

_____

We like to go to God all cleaned up. God likes us to come to Him as we are, knowing our true state, because He already knows it anyway. **In our true state, He meets us, answers us, and brings solutions to our impossibilities.**

ACT ON IT!

- Have a moment of quiet time with God. Physically lift up your hands to Him and tell of the things you desire for Him to take control of. Let go of all inhibition and run to your Father who loves you and wants to take care of you. Allow Him to do the impossible for you.

- Make a list of things that look impossible. Write them down. Pray over them. Burn them up as a sign that you no longer believe they are impossible.

Eve's Angels

Finding Your Voice

Finding Your Voice

Week One: Breaking the Curse

It's not a very popular teaching, but God is both male and female. **Read Genesis 1:27.** God is neither man nor woman, because He's Spirit, which does not have gender, however it has essence, and essence has to do with function.

The question is what part of God is female in function? We find that answer when we look at ourselves. The part of God that is female is the part that births forth. There is great responsibility and power in this, which is why the enemy works to steal a woman's voice and what she was created to proclaim.

The Bride of Christ is also feminine in essence, and therefore births forth for the King. How do we do this? Through our words. Through our voice. In order to do this however, we have to find out what message we were sent here to deliver.

Read Together Genesis 3:1-4

Now the serpent was more crafty than any of the wild animals the LORD God had made. He said to the woman, "Did God really say, 'You must not eat from

any tree in the garden'?" The woman said to the serpent, "We may eat fruit from the trees in the garden, but God did say, 'You must not eat fruit from the tree that is in the middle of the garden, and you must not touch it, or you will die.' "You will not surely die," the serpent said to the woman. "For God knows that when you eat of it your eyes will be opened, and you will be like God, knowing good and evil."

Satan was trying to *deceive* Eve into being what she *already* was, but in a *counterfeit* way.

What are the lies being told to the woman?

_____

_____

_____

_____

_____

What truths are being distorted by the enemy in this conversation?

_____

_____

_____

_____

_____

God was the creator of the world. He spoke the world into existence. Eve was made in the image of God and also could create through speaking. When Satan approached her, he convinced her that she needed to do something to be what she already was.

She already was like God. When Adam and Eve fell, they received physical, decaying bodies. Eve was now under a curse.

Read and Write Out Genesis 3:16

_____

_____

_____

_____

_____

Now, the only way Eve can create is with the help of her husband to make children. A man must speak on her behalf. She can no longer create through speaking, because Satan stole her voice.

In what ways has your voice been stolen or stifled?

_____

_____

_____

_____

_____

Good News! God broke this curse when Mary became pregnant not through a man, but with the spoken Word. The angel came and spoke to her that she was to become pregnant with Jesus. At this time, Mary only knew of the natural way to create under the curse.

Read and Write Out Luke 1:34

_____

_____

_____

_____

_____

Mary has never been with a man, but now she becomes pregnant through the Holy Spirit.

Read and Write Out John 1:1

_____

_____

_____

_____

_____

Mary got her voice back by getting pregnant with The Word. She gave birth to Jesus in the natural, but she is our prototype for what we are to do in the Spirit. We can birth through words as we speak truth with our mouths.

EVERY WOMAN HAS THE POWER TO GIVE BIRTH TO A WORD THAT CAN CHANGE THE WORLD.

ACT ON IT!

- Do you feel like you have lost your voice? Why? Who took it from you?

_____

_____

_____

_____

_____

- Identify places/times in your life when the enemy has tried to tell you to become something you already were.

_____

_____

_____

_____

_____

- Who does God tell you that you are? Write down key words that pop into your head as you ask God to tell you the truth of who He says you are.

KEY WORDS THAT DESCRIBE YOU FROM GOD

Finding Your Voice

Week Two: Sarah & Hagar

Sarah and Hagar were both women who conceived a child for Abraham. Sarah is a prototype of birthing in the Spirit and Hagar of birthing in the natural.

Abraham was promised that he would have a son and then Jesus spoke that promise into Sarah. When Hagar became pregnant with Abraham's son, Ishmael, it was done naturally.

Abraham had two children; Isaac was birthed through a promise and Ishmael was birthed in the flesh. Let's explore the important difference of laboring in the flesh versus conceiving in the Spirit.

Read Together Galatians 4:22-26

"For it is written that Abraham had two sons, one by the slave woman and the other by the free woman. [23] His son by the slave woman was born in the ordinary way; but his son by the free woman was born as the result of a promise. These things may be taken figuratively, for the women represent two covenants. One covenant is from Mount Sinai and bears children who are to be slaves: This is Hagar. Now Hagar stands for Mount Sinai in Arabia and corresponds to the present city of Jerusalem, because she is in slavery with her

children. But the Jerusalem that is above is free, and she is our mother."

When you birth in the Spirit, you are bringing forth a word from God, which brings *freedom*.

How can you tell the difference between creating in the flesh and the Spirit? What are some of the fruits that you will see from both creating in our own strength and will and when we create in the Spirit?

_____

_____

_____

_____

_____

Now Sarah, being very far along in years (she was old), was in all human comprehension too old to have children and she was also barren having given birth to no other children in her earlier years. Her voice and longing was stifled when she was not able to procreate (and if you remember, we are creators by the nature that God originally intended us to have). However, God gives Sarah her voice back, even as an old woman! Genesis 18 tells the story of what happened to Abraham's wife and how she gets her voice back:

Three visitors show up at Abraham's tent, and he recognizes them as two angels with the pre-incarnate form of Jesus Christ so he immediately starts to serve them.

Jesus tells Abraham that within a year, Sarah will have a child. Sarah, being very old and no longer having the ability to conceive naturally, was impregnated with a word. When Jesus **spoke** the promise to Abraham, Sarah got her voice back and she **laughed**. *God told Abraham that his child's name would be Isaac, which means laughter.*

The next verse in the passage from Galatians quotes **Isaiah 54:1,** which says,

"Sing, O barren woman,
   you who never bore a child;
burst into song, shout for joy,
   you who were never in labor;
because more are the children of the desolate woman
   than of her who has a husband,"
says the LORD.

Sarah could have tried everything humanly possible to conceive and have a child, however, when we try to create out of our own strength, apart from God's will, we are laboring in the flesh and the result is always less than satisfying.

Labor is part of the curse that was given in Genesis. Now, a woman who is not conceiving in the third dimension, but in the Spirit, can bear more fruit than a woman who is creating in the flesh.

Having physical children is not a curse, but now, women are no longer limited to only creating physically because they can give birth to the Word.

ACT ON IT!

- Pray and ask the LORD to show you places where you are laboring in the flesh when you need to be conceiving in the Spirit. Can you recall a time when you were conceiving in the Spirit?

Where have you been laboring in the flesh?	Where have you been conceiving in the Spirit?
1.	1.
2.	2.
3.	3.
4.	4.

- What do you have a passion for? Write it down. What would you like to see happen with the passion that you have?

_____

_____

_____

_____

_____

Finding Your Voice

Week Three: Seek and You Will Find

Directions: We want you to take this week and seek out the scriptures for answers to questions we have discussed over the last months. Use a concordance, website, and each other to find scriptures to back up each of the following questions and thoughts. Ask your leader for help!

1. When you find your voice it delivers you from others' opinions, because it's not just what you say, it's who you are and the way you are.

Scriptures:_____

_____

_____

_____

_____

2. How does God express Himself in you?

Scriptures:_____

_____

_____

_____

3. *What do we do to stifle this expression and voice that God has given us?*

Scriptures:_____

_____

_____

_____

_____

4. *Fulfilling your destiny means finding and expressing 'your truth' that God gave only you.*

Scriptures:_____

_____

_____

_____

_____

5. *Jesus knew who He was- He didn't have identity issues Jesus said He doesn't do and say anything He doesn't see or hear the Father doing*

Scriptures:_____

_____

_____

_____

_____

6. Finding your voice is becoming who you were created to be. What were you put on this earth to say and do?

Scriptures:_____

_____

_____

_____

_____

ACT ON IT!

- Come ready next week to celebrate the last year of studying God's Word together. Bring a few testimonies and ideas to share as you encourage each other in the next place God is taking your group

Finding Your Voice

Week Four: Speak Out

We want you to take this final week and share stories with the group about the last twelve months you have spent together. Celebrate your successes and the truth God has revealed to you. Pray for one another as you continue on in your journey.

Discussion Questions:

1. What has God revealed to you during the last year?

2. When has God been faithful to you over these months together? Take some time and have each person share a testimony of God's faithfulness.

3. How have you changed from glory to glory while studying God's word?

Write down one memory that you can look back to and recall God changing your heart and life over this time.

_____
_____
_____
_____
_____

Thank you for taking this journey. I hope you were able to find out more about yourself, more about the Kingdom, and more about how much God really loves you.

We are all in different places in our process as humans, but God knew you were going to read this before I ever wrote it. He had you specifically in mind.

I hope you heard Him, felt Him, saw Him, and are closer to Him than you ever have been.

Know that you are not alone in your process. Please email and let us know what this has done for you, questions you have, and ways this has changed your life at: info@evesangels.org.

God is closer than you think.

Blessings to you on your journey.

Anny